BUFFALO

. . . and Indians
on the Great Plains

OTHER BOOKS BY THE AUTHOR

Tame the Restless Wind
A Serpent for a Dove
Beyond the Schoolhouse
Crossroads at San Felipe
Historic San Antonio and the
      Border Country (co-author)
Historic Churches of Texas (co-author)

OTHER BOOKS BY THE ARTIST

The Donkey Sat Down
Papacito
Indians Who Lived in Texas
Queen Cat
Make a Joyful Noise
5 books in Let's Remember series on
      Texas History
The Thirteen Colonies
The Story of Texas
Wildflowers of Texas

NOEL GRISHAM
Illustrated by Betsy Warren

BUFFALO

. . . and Indians

on the Great Plains

EAKIN PRESS
Austin, Texas

To John David,
Amy Aiken and Dennis Natho Ellington,
grandchildren of the author.

FIRST EDITION

Published in the United States of America
By Eakin Press, P.O. Box 23066, Austin, Texas 73735

ISBN 0-89015-470-8

2

CONTENTS

Where Buffalo Once Roamed

Buffalo were in America long before Christopher Columbus came in the year 1492. Millions and millions of the huge, shaggy animals roamed over the wide prairies of the Great Plains. They fed on thick grasses which covered these flat lands. In the middle of America, the Great Plains area stretches all the way from Canada down into Texas.

During summer months, buffalo herds had plenty of wild grasses to eat. To find grass in winter months, a buffalo cleared a path in the snow with his large head.

When food was scarce, some of the herds moved farther south where grass grew in the wintertime. When large herds came together, it looked as though a great, dark blanket was covering the ground as far as the eye could see.

The first white man to see American buffalo was Cabeza de Vaca. He was a Spaniard who came to the plains of Texas sometime in 1533. Cabeza called the buffalo "Indian cattle" and "oxen."

Later, when French explorers came to America, they called the strange animals "les Boeufs." From this French name comes the English word "buffalo."

HOW INDIANS HUNTED THE BUFFALO

Wherever there were buffalo, Indians could be found close by. Indians who lived on the Great Plains found out that the buffalo could give them everything they needed — food, clothing, shelter and tools. Since their lives depended on these animals, they learned to be good hunters.

The best months for hunting were in June, July and August. Buffalo were fat from eating summer grasses, and their dark brown fur was beginning to grow thick for winter-time.

While hunting buffalo, the Indians walked or ran because there were no horses to ride in early days of America. They had to be fast runners to keep up with the buffalo who could run 35 to 45 miles per hour over a long distance. However, Indians were so strong, they could travel on foot for many hours without getting tired.

Buffalo were easily frightened by the sight of human beings. When they saw people, they often stampeded and ran wildly across the land. Indians were careful not to scare them. Because buffalo were not afraid of wolves, a hunter sometimes covered himself with a wolf skin. In this disguise, he could crawl close enough to shoot stone-tipped arrows or throw a spear into a buffalo's side. He aimed for a spot just behind the shoulder blade in order to kill the animal more quickly.

Hunters also found a way to kill more than one animal at a time. Surrounding three sides of a herd, many Indians ran and shouted to drive the buffalo towards a steep cliff. The excited animals stampeded and were not able to stop running when they reached the edge of the cliff. Large numbers of them crashed to the ground below. Men waiting there could subdue them easily.

Another use was made of "the surround." Hunters formed a circle around a small herd and drove the animals into a corral made of logs. When the gate was closed, the buffalo were kept in the pen until they were needed.

After horses were brought to America by Spanish explorers, Indians on the Plains learned how to be fine horsemen. By the early 1700s, they found that hunting buffalo could be done better from horseback. Armed with bow and arrows and a long spear, the hunter was able to ride close enough to a running animal to wound it with arrows. After losing blood, the buffalo became too tired to run. When the hunter thrust a spear into its shoulder, the buffalo came crashing to the ground.

With horses, buffalo, and the freedom to move across the land, Plains Indians felt they had everything they needed for a good life. They were sure there would always be plenty of buffalo for their families to eat so that they could live on the Great Plains forever.

USING BUFFALO FOR FOOD

Buffalo hunts were often far away from the Indian campsites. Since the animals were too large to be carried a great distance after they had been killed, they were skinned and cut into small pieces on the spot. All of the parts were packed in the skins and tied to a V-shaped framework called a "travois" (travoy). A dog or horse pulled the loaded travois back to camp.

All members of an Indian tribe gathered to feast on the buffalo meat brought back to camp. The best parts of the meat were roasted over an open fire., No one ate until after a tribal member raised a piece of meat to the sky and thanked both the buffalo and the Great Spirit for the food and hides given to his people.

14

15

After the feast, women cut smaller pieces of the meat into thin strips. These strips were hung on a long rack to dry in the sun for several days or they were smoked dry over a fire. Called "jerky," the dried meat could be kept for a long time without spoiling. Each warrior carried jerky in his saddlebags to use as food during long hunting trips. It was a favorite food and even Indian babies were given jerky to chew.

Another important food for Indians was *pemmican* —
a kind of sausage. Dried flakes of buffalo meat were
pounded into shreds between stones and put into skin
bags. After wild berries and nuts were added, melted fat
from a bear or buffalo was poured over the mixture. When
the fat hardened, pemmican kept without spoiling for as
long as three years. Because it provided food during times
of the year when buffalo were scarce, it was highly valued
by the Indians.

How Buffalo Hides Were Prepared

After preserving meat for food, Indian women immediately began to prepare buffalo hides into a kind of leather. The skins were tied on to a pole framework to be dried and stretched. Using a sharp rock or buffalo bone, the women scraped hair and pieces of fat from the skins. After pegging the hides to the ground, women pounded and rubbed them with smooth stones. The more it was pounded, the softer the skin became. Rubbing bear or buffalo grease into the hides made them more pliable and water-proof. It took many days of hard work to prepare buffalo hides, but they could be used for a long time before they wore out.

MAKING A TEPEE

Plains Indians lived in homes called *tepees*. Twenty long poles and fifteen to twenty buffalo skins were needed to make a large tepee. After punching holes with a sharp stone-awl into the edges of the hides, women sewed them together with heavy thread made of buffalo sinews. The skins were then thrown over the tall poles which had been tied together at the top and spread into a cone shape. An opening with flaps was left at the top as a smokehole. The flaps could be closed when it rained.

At the bottom, pegs were driven into the hides to hold the tepee to the ground. Rocks and dirt were piled around the bottom to keep out wind and cold. An opening which always faced to the East was covered with a stiff piece of hide for use as a door. Tepee skins were usually decorated with paintings and designs done by the owner. His designs were never copied unless he gave permission.

Tepees made of the thick buffalo hides lasted a long time. When the Indians moved camp, they wrapped the hides around the tall poles after packing food and belongings inside. The tepees were carried along and set up at each new campsite. It took only fifteen minutes for a woman to put up a tepee and five minutes to take one down.

Clothes And Ornaments

In wintertime, the hair of the buffalo grew very thick. Indians kept the warm furry skins to wear as robes and raincoats or to use as beds and hammocks.

Smaller pieces of the buffalo hides were cut to be sturdy soles for moccasins. The tough soles were sewn to tops made of softened deerskin. Dresses, leggings and vests were also made of the hides.

Decorated with designs, a luggage case sewn from buffalo skin was owned by each Indian. Called a *parfleche,* it held the Indian's belongings and was carried over the shoulder or attached to the saddle of a horse.

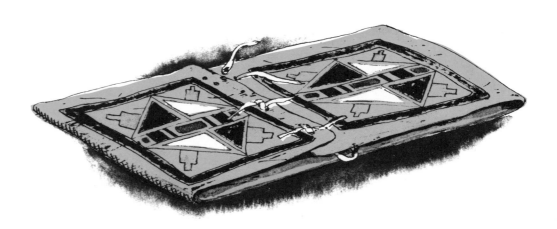

Chiefs often wore the head of a buffalo as a sign of great honor and protection. Indian men wore them during dances which were held to celebrate a buffalo hunt. On their shields, the beard of a buffalo was hung as decoration.

23

TOOLS, WEAPONS AND
MUSICAL INSTRUMENTS

Every part of the buffalo was useful to the Plains
Indians. Bones became scraping tools or were carved for
use as needles. An awl of sharpened bone was used for
punching holes in thick skins to make sewing easier. The
wide blade of the buffalo shoulder became a spade when
tied to a long handle. Arrow heads were also carved from
bones.

A large hide stretched over a tub-like frame became a
useful boat in crossing rivers. It was called a *bull boat*.

Glue was made by boiling the hooves, and a buffalo horn could form a knife handle. Horns were also used as drinking cups, spoons, and as cases for carrying paints and gun powder. Soft, porous hip-bones became paint brushes after they were chewed.

Powder Horn

Hoe

Spoon

Paint Brush

Knife Handle

Cooking Paunch

Cooking pots were fashioned from stiff hides. Buffalo sinews were put to use as threads and bow strings. Tail hairs were woven into ropes, halters, belts and ornaments. The bladder of a buffalo was useful as a water bottle. Rib bones became runners for sleds.

Child's Sled

Of great importance to an Indian warrior was his rawhide shield. A piece of thick hide was tied securely to a large hoop and was decorated with designs and feathers and buffalo tails and beards. The shield was held by a warrior to ward off enemy arrows or bullets during a battle.

Pieces of wet hide were stretched over a wooden saddle frame that had been padded with buffalo hair. When the skin dried, it stuck closely to the padded frame and made a saddle more comfortable for the horse and rider.

Man's Saddle

Woman's Saddle

Fly Swatter

Tails of the buffalo were also useful as fly swatters.

When white men who were traders came to the Plains, Indians gave them buffalo hides in exchange for guns, cloth and trinkets. The traders shipped the hides to factories in Europe where they were made into strong leather belts used in machinery.

Even the bones left on the prairies were useful. Dried bones of buffalo were gathered by white farmers and sold to factories in American cities. They were then ground into bone meal for fertilizers.

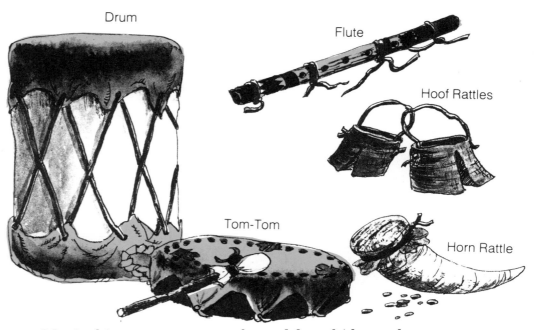

Drum

Flute

Hoof Rattles

Tom-Tom

Horn Rattle

Musical instruments were formed from hides and bones. When holes were bored into a slender, hollow bone, it was blown as a flute. Hollowed-out hooves or horns filled with pebbles made musical rattles.

Buffalo skins laced to wooden frames made drums and tom-toms.

THE WHITE BUFFALO

Of all the millions of buffalo on the Plains, only a few white animals were ever sighted. Called an "albino," the rare white creature was held in awe by the Indians. They believed that a white buffalo skin gave magical powers to the whole tribe.

A warrior thought that he would be protected in battle if he wore one of the white hides. Medicine men believed that if they wore a white buffalo robe, they would have special healing powers. By sacrificing the animal to the Great Spirit, Indians thought it would bring health and success to all the tribe. They also believed that the white buffalo could change itself into a white hawk, a gray fox, or even a beautiful woman.

Valued as a great prize, a white buffalo could be traded for as many as fifteen fine horses.

Indian Buffalo Dances

When white men came to the Great Plains in the 1800s, they destroyed the huge buffalo herds. Leaving the meat to rot on the prairies, they took only the hides and furs. They shipped them to factories in eastern states for the making of hats, clothing and blankets.

The Indians knew that their lives were in danger without the herds of buffalo to sustain them. Although they fought many battles to keep white hunters from killing all the buffalo, Indians could not win against the superior weapons of the white man.

White Cloud, a Sioux Indian who lived many years ago, spoke these sad words: "Wherever the whites are established, the buffalo is gone and the red hunters die of hunger."

By performing dances, Indians hoped that buffalo herds would once again cover the prairies. They believed that friends and families of long ago would come down the Ghost Road to join with them in hunting the buffalo on earth.

Hoping to bring back the lost days of the great buffalo hunts, Indians of the Plains developed the Ghost Dance. Wearing painted Ghost shirts, men and women joined hands in a large circle to dance and sing for many days. Sometimes they fell into trances and told of seeing visions. Some said they traveled the "Ghost Road" in the sky that led to the Great Spirit. To them, the Milky Way was the Ghost Road.

But the buffalo were gone. The few stray animals that were left were not enough to feed the starving Indians. They were forced by white men to live enclosed on reservations so that white families could settle on the Great Plains where the buffalo had once roamed. All that remained were the tales told of hunting the great animal.

Today, stories of those days are told only in books. All children who read the stories will help to keep alive the memories of the Indian hunters and the great buffalo so that they will never be forgotten.

SOME WORDS TO KNOW

rawhide
preserve
hammock
reservation
galaxy
Milky Way
albino
stampede
travois
jerky
pemmican
tepee
sinews
moccasins
parfleche
bull boat

BIBLIOGRAPHY

Title	Author	Publisher
Indians of the Plains	Sheppard	Watts
How the Plains Indians Lived	Fichter	McKay
Indians of the Southwest	Baldwin	Putnam's
Return of the Buffalo	Scott-Sweet	Putnam's
Frontier America		Museum of Fine Arts Boston
The Indians of Texas	Newcomb	UT Press
Indians of the Plains	American Heritage	Golden Press
Comanches	Fehrenbach	Knopf
Indians	Tunis	World

ABOUT THE AUTHOR

Noel Grisham was a public school superintendent for thirty-two years, the last twenty-two years in Round Rock Independent School District part of which is in the city of Austin. He has been a Lieutenant Governor of the Texas Oklahoma District of Kiwanis International. He has served on numerous state committees and has written numerous articles for state and national journals. He is a former member of the Texas House of Representatives and a member of the board of directors of the First National Bank of Round Rock.

ABOUT THE ARTIST

Betsy Warren lives in Austin where she and her husband have raised four children. In addition to illustrating many text and trade books, she has also written fourteen books for young readers.